talking
to the Moon

POETRY AND PROSE

© 2023 Talking to the Moon by Brandy Lane

Editor: Reena Doss

All rights reserved.
Printed in the United States of America.

No part of this book may be used, stored in a system retrieval system, or transmitted, in any form or any means—by electronic, mechanical, photocopying, recording, or reproduced in any manner whatsoever—without written permission from the author, except in the case of brief quotations embodied in critical articles and reviews.

Published in the United States of America
by Where Beautiful Inks LLC

Fort Wayne, Indiana

ISBN: 978-1-7363268-4-8

Library of Congress Control Number: 2023914198

All pictures throughout this book are available through
Canva and Canva Pro.

Author's Note

For the selenophiles.

Or for anyone who has
ever looked at the moon
and saw the face
of the one they adore
looking back.

Dedication

MY DARLING DRAGON,

*I will forever look at you
as though you hold the stars
and the moon in your eyes.*

A Thank You to My Muse

I suppose my eyes are often toward the sky, constantly searching for a sign that you are still there. It is a happy occasion when I can see the moon in the bright blue atmosphere of day—playing peek-a-boo. I pretend it is you, smiling down at me.

Nighttime inevitably comes, the shadows creep up on me and the moon's glow lightens my path as you have lightened my burdens. All I need to do is walk in the soft light and think of all the beautiful moments we have shared, the laughter, the sweet conversations. And even though they are now memories, your words still affect me every single day.

On the occasion of the new moon, the times when I cannot see the brilliant orb in the sky, I must remember that even though I cannot see it, it is still there. Much like you, not being able to see you has been hard, and lonely... but remembering you are still out there somewhere, calms my spirit.

You gave me a new purpose when I had none. You taught me how to find my inner strength, and have been right there for me through what could have been the worst years of my life. I wouldn't have gotten through them without your friendship.

I will always love you,

Brandy

Contents

Collide 3
Conjure 4
Who He is to Me 6
End of Day 8
Void 11
Ellipsis 12
Tarnished 14
Afar 16
Eclipse 18
Memories 20
Stardust 22
Glow 24
Stargazing 26
Summer's End 28
Sun and Moon 30
Wish 32
Need 33
He 34
Company 36
Luna 38
Blanket of Stars 40

talking
to the Moon

POETRY AND PROSE

Talking to the Moon

Collide

Burnished silver turned to grey
like the love we once had.
Used to shine like the moonlight,
but now a dull matte.

Wanting nothing more
than to take that trip
one last time.

Holding hands, laughing
over the blare of the radio—
looking into the future
and leaving everything behind.

Where did the time go?
What if we just kept right on going?
What if we skip the road home
where we cannot be together?

I suppose we must wait
until we can trade
our wheels in for wings
before our souls can once again,
collide.

Brandy Lane

Conjure

It's not that I expect the morning,
not in the way that I think I can
conjure its light.
Nor do I demand the moon—
in its diminishing smile,
or whilst full and bright.

But if they were to disappear?
You can imagine what chaos would ensue!
I suppose in my head and my heart,
those are the feelings I have about you.

No, I never expect it,
because I've grown to accept
each moment as it comes.
Though some days
the clouds obscure the light,
whether the moon or sun—

they're both still there!

The sun still shines in all its glorious ways,
and the moon sometimes smiles its toothy grin,
reflecting the beaming rays.

Talking to the Moon

Of course,
there are nights the moon is quiet—
no grin, no light.

Still there, just hiding up in the darkness,
right there in plain sight.

You are my moon in its many phases,
hanging in my atmosphere
and over the course of time I've learned,
I shall not fret nor fear.

Even when you are dark,
I see you.

I will forever want you in my gravity
and in that, there's no denial.

I will even love you on the days
there are no reasons—
to smile.

Brandy Lane

Who He is to Me

To me, he is the morning light,
He brightens my day,
no matter the mood.

He's my moon at night,
guiding me through the dark.

He's my rhythm and my rhyme,
my reason to sing and to write.

He's my love affair,
the one I'd give up heaven
and go through hell for.

Talking to the Moon

Brandy Lane

End of Day

A chill in the air,
after seventy degrees
under sunny skies of blue.

A sweater to wear,
now a much cooler breeze
the skies are a lavender hue.

A sliver of moon,
smiles at me in the dusk—
I smile back at him.

I wonder if
you're smiling back at him too,
as this day grows dim.

Talking to the Moon

Brandy Lane

Void

One day the sun, she ceased to shine...
the moon declared, "Oh how divine!
Without her here, the sky's all mine!"

He settled in the sky real low,
feigning star of his own show,
unaware he had no glow.

Without his counterpart of day—
there was no light left to display,
not one solitary ray.

He just sat there, cold and still,
swallowing that bitter pill—
her void is something he can't fill.

Brandy Lane

Ellipsis

I used to sleep in dragon's wings
wrapped tightly 'round my chest...
Just like a hug, I'd snuggle down,
and close my eyes to rest.

My dragon is no longer here,
I left him back at home...
As solitary creatures are,
they just don't care to roam.

So now I sleep on blankets, soft
and downy are the pillows...
I dream that I can fly on clouds
in undulating billows.

Talking to the Moon

I hope to find my dragon there,
deep within my dreams...
So I can hug him once again,
in the moonlight's beams.

Someday I'll see him in real life,
it is my heart's desire...
Because my love has now been forged
within that dragon's fire.

My soul is longingly in pause—
love hidden by eclipses...
Until someday we meet again,
it's waiting in ellipsis.

Brandy Lane

Tarnished

Sterling were my linings—
the shiny silver outlines
that turned the greys beautiful.

One by one,
I polished the clouds
that loomed inside
my melancholy mind…
They sparkled as moonlight
on a midnight lake.

I forgot that silver
T A R N I S H E S.

A cloudy haze,
dingier than what was there prior…
I struggle now to find
the beauty within.

All of the work I had done,
all of the magnificence—
now shrouded in black.

Talking to the Moon

Brandy Lane

Afar

I cannot wait until the day
that I can look upon your face again—
to gaze into those eyes
and get lost in another dimension.

I long for the moment
to graze your palm,
as my fingers slip inside your grasp—
snuggled up on the couch,
by your side.

I was so lucky to have you near me
even if for such a short time.

Those moments
have such power over me
that the mere memories of them
bring amazing comfort.

Talking to the Moon

You are still home to my soul.

I greet each day
with anticipation of returning.

For now,

let me be your moon in the darkness.

Allow me to be in the distance—
smiling down on you.

Feel my gravity tugging your heartstrings—
playing them like a melody
that brings your spirit peace.

Let me love you from afar.

Brandy Lane

Eclipse

We're going in circles
at different paces,
but my darling, it doesn't matter!

The sun and the moon,
in their concentricity,
don't seem to mind.
At some point,
Luna will eclipse Sol,
turn face, and kiss him.

She isn't even shy about it,
and has no need
to doubt him in his travels.
Why do you think
she glows so beautifully?
She reflects his love,
shouting in beams—
reflecting onto
the darkened world,
below.

Talking to the Moon

He carries the day and she holds the night while it slumbers.

Brandy Lane

Memories

Before the sun awakens
and the moon goes back to bed,
I wanted to jot down
the ideas in my head.

Like dandelion seeds,
they're scattered to and fro,
trying to find a fertile place
where they can stop to grow.

Many thoughts are wasted,
they never see the light—
others birth the dreams
I have throughout the night.

Some are rather beautiful,
some colorful, some vast;
others are just random memories
of my distant past.

Talking to the Moon

They drift like snowflakes,
falling, dancing all around,
before they slowly, carefully,
lie upon the ground.

I see the sky is brightening,
ready for the day
but not yet for me—I'm tired.
Back upon my bed, I lay.

Maybe I'll catch a coupl'a winks and
blow dandelions more,
or perhaps jot ideas down
so they'll last forevermore.

Brandy Lane

Stardust

May angels kiss your cheeks
as your mind wanders to sleep;
may stardust line your lashes,
may you slumber long and deep.

May all your dreams be hopeful,
and get you through the night;
may they stoke the very fires
of your soul, burning bright.

Talking to the Moon

I will always love you,
you're forever part of me,
and all I wish for you is that,
life makes you happy.

Brandy Lane

Glow

I like the moments in the silence:
the ones where all I can feel is you—
without even touching.

The moments where I sense
the tingling electricity
that radiates from the nuclei
of your being.
I can sense you in the universe—
like gravity,
an ever-pulling magnetic force
that tugs at everything I am.

It's exhausting not colliding with you.
I am forever stuck in your gravity!
You pull my emotions like the tide,
the oceans within me rise and fall.
I long for you, yet you hover,
as the moon...

Contently orbiting.

Pleasantly smiling.

Reflectively musing.

Talking to the Moon

*I am in love with the moon,
and the moon loves me.
He loves me so very much
that he watches from a distance,
bathing me in his soft glow.*

Brandy Lane

Stargazing

To wander in the moonlight with you
and gaze at the sky as I often do...
A glowing green from Aurora streaks—
along with a night owl's hungry shrieks.
We sit down by the fire's glow
with sticks for toasting marshmallow.

The sky soon clears to the darkest of blacks
as we lie upon blankets on our backs
and stare up at the Milky Way—
no need for any words to say.
I take your hand and hold it tight,
as we lay there throughout the night.

You look at me with those blue eyes,
more lost than I had realized.
After all what can we do
with this love 'tween me and you?
There's is no reason, or no rhyme...
Perhaps if we could turn back time?

Talking to the Moon

I suppose as we just lie in wait
and wonder how we scorned our fate
to have a love so pure and sweet
but only for our souls to meet—
only for my heart to know,
just how much I love you so.

This bittersweet decadence
fills me with much recompense!
I will hold you in my heart, so soft
so you can always stay aloft—
my lost love has now been found.
Alas, this love cannot be bound.

What if I escaped these chains,
if our love had no refrains?
What if I could be with you
and feast upon this love so true?
That is where I long to be,
right next to you, you next to me.

Brandy Lane

Summer's End

Sitting in the dark,
the pale moon-glow washes over me.
Cool breezes whisk by,
summer's days are nearing an end.

The cicadas have finished their serenade;
it's the cricket's turn to shine
as they play their leg violins fervently.

The dampness of the recent rainy days
remains on the earth;
a sweet petrichor—
that mostly perfumes
the acrid blend
of stale old smoke and musty leaves
that fills the air.

Talking to the Moon

I'm looking forward to autumn,
the cooler nights,
the amber sun with its light waning—
slightly earlier each night.

The leaves,
in their chlorophyll-deprived state,
will turn bright reds and yellows
in their last hurrah before their final lilt—
to the ground below.

Brandy Lane

Sun and Moon

If I could capture the sunshine,
I would place it outside your window
to brighten your days and disposition.

As far as the moon?

I'd put a pull chain on it
just so you could turn it off
when you wanted
to see all of the stars
and turn it on
whenever you felt alone
at night.

You could adjust it
to waxing or waning,
so you could take a midnight stroll,
or sit quietly next to your one true love
and watch it move
across the night sky.

Wish

And although she couldn't see him,
she new that he was there,
just like the moon in the sky
when it is new.

She saw the stars
and made a wish,
in hopes
to see him soon.

Brandy Lane

Talking to the Moon

Need

What if I've realized
I need you?

Like the Earth
needs the Sun?

Like the tides
need the Moon?

Like the flowers
need the bees?

Brandy Lane

He

I wonder if God was reminiscing
about the day He formed the oceans,
when he put so much depth into your eyes.

I'm curious if He pondered the
height of the redwoods
when he graced your stature,
or if he fashioned your hair after
the silver moonbeams
on the clearest of winter nights.

I'm curious how he chiseled your calves
like marble and delicately crafted your nose
as if it were clay, yet your earlobes
are as lilies, supple and firm.

I am amazed at how He fashioned your soul
to be as the stars, shining from the heavens;
your personality twinkling like the Milky Way
in the vastness of the universe.

I am fascinated by the care He took
while piecing you together,
entwining grace and charm
with strength and intelligence
in such a beautiful way.

Talking to the Moon

I cannot help but marvel at your mind
and the intricacies within.
You are more beautiful to me
than any of the wonders of the world,
and I want nothing more than to explore.

Brandy Lane

Company

*Just as the moon
will never be mine,
yet I have sat many nights
in its company.*

Brandy Lane

Luna

Restless...
The cocoon has become stifling!
Is this how the moth feels upon her reawakening?
Is it hunger that drives her?
The taste of sweet nectar from moonflowers
or the suffocating feeling
that overwhelms her to break free?
Pressure that used to bring comfort,
now squeezing so tight
that escaping is the only way to survive.
She squirms and shimmies to no avail,
captive in a trap
she made for herself to keep others out,
now desperate to escape
lest she be entombed for eternity.
She has no room to move,
she bites the hardened silk by her mandible
and begins to tear it,
little by little.

Talking to the Moon

Hours later, she is free!
Exhausted, crumpled... but alive.
She rests in the glow of the moonlight—
so beautiful, yet not many will ever see.
She hides in darkness,
never to see the light of day.
Her wings outstretched,
are rather large and cumbersome
but are much more useful for
gliding on the subtle breeze
than a smaller pair, not to mention...
the silence.
No one hears her in the stillness
as she floats from bough to bark.
She carries her beauty in darkness
and only the lucky will see.

Brandy Lane

I WANT TO BE UNDER A BLANKET OF STARS

with
the pines
all around, as
if guarding me.

Frost just t r y i n g
to BITE my nose

as the campfire

dances

in the solitude
of night.

Also Published in

So grateful for the editors and publishers that have included the following poems in their anthologies and magazines. The poems, many times in their rawest and earliest versions, appeared as follows.

Sun and Moon was published in **Where Beautiful Loves** as well as **Bloom Magazine** by Red Penguin Books

Wish was first published in **Where Beautiful Loves**

Poetry 365 by RDW (both abridged and unabridged editions) for November, December, January, February, March, April, May, and June, and special editions of *Creator*, *Hope*, and *Self Portrait* editions.

Red Penguin Books has published her pieces in *'Tis the Season's*, *The Flower Shop on the Corner*, *The Ocean Waves*, and *Bloom Issue 2* magazine.

Clarendon House Publications published her poems in their *Poetica 2* and *Poetica 3* anthologies.

Ink Gladiators Press' anthologies of *The Rise and Fall of Chimera's* and *Gray, We Hide our Colors Within*.

Indie Blu(e) *Publishing* just published a mental health piece in *Through the Looking Glass: Reflecting on Madness and Chaos Within*, and their newest anthology, *But You Don't Look Sick: The Real Life Adventures of Fibro Bitches, Lupus Warriors, and Other Superheroes Battling Invisible Illness*.

300 South Media Group has published her in *As Darkness Falls* and features her first flash fiction piece in *Sunset Rain*.

Train River Poetry has published her in *Poetry 7*.

Who's Who of Emerging Writers by Sweetycat Press.

Harness Magazine in their November 2022 issue.

Silent Spark Press *Amazing Poetry Volume 13*, 2023.

Brandy Lane

"If I could only lasso all of my drifting thoughts with a pen and ensnare them in the fibers of paper!"

About the Author

Brandy Lane has lived most of her life in Indiana and Colorado, where she resides with her husband and four children. She published her first book, **Where Beautiful Loves**, in December 2020 under her imprint, **Where Beautiful Inks**. Just after the release of her first book, she discovered anthologies as an option for publishing and has since had poetry pieces included in over three dozen publications. In 2023, she curated and edited, **Winter, A Poetic Anthology** which is a collaboration of 25 poets from all over the world. It spent 5 days at #1 in New Releases in Anthologies on Amazon.

A hopeless romantic, Brandy draws inspiration mainly from nature, but also from human connection. Her poetry is much like her personality, showing vulnerability as well as strength. The muse that she writes to is someone who taught her she is worthy of love, that she is "enough" and yes, "sometimes more than enough." She finds beauty in every situation, which sometimes is her greatest curse.

In her spare time, she loves spending time outdoors in the mountains, taking in the sublime views. She also loves a good board game, and video chatting with her favorite friends all over the world.

Brandy can be found online: on Instagram @wherebeautifullives and Facebook @Where Beautiful Lives

"I'll find you in the dark because I'm the girl who loves to stay lost amongst the midnight stars caught up with moonbeams in a lantern trying to find my way back home."

About the Editor

Reena Doss considers writing to be her first voice of expression, followed closely by art and creativity. Through the encouraging platform provided by the Instagram community, she reclaimed her lost voices, evolved a few others and discovered new ones along the way. This has redeemed her trust that consistent Hope, Faith and Love in what is true ignites what is impossible to occur. Her adoration for her beloved Weaver, the Celestial Sky, Nature and her fellow Earthians has given her immeasurable courage to endure every season with a resilience born from battles overcome. She also showcases her artistic talents at His Wild, which features her digital paintings and shares her passion for children's literature at The Pickleton Universe by working on kid lit books for the future. Reena is also the Founder of Ink Gladiators Press where she publishes theme based work in anthologies under the names—Our Earthians Community Group and Translations Of Hope, reviews self-published books and recommends self-publishing services at IGP Ship. Overall, her voices are a reflection of her personality, life story and unwavering faith.

Currently, she resides in Bangalore, India but loves traveling to far-off places inside her head and sometimes, in the world that others call real. You can try and catch her on Instagram at reenadossauthor but it may not always be possible as she is generally off on adventures chasing dragons, phoenixes and mermaids down for stories. www.reenadoss.com

Other books by Brandy Lane:

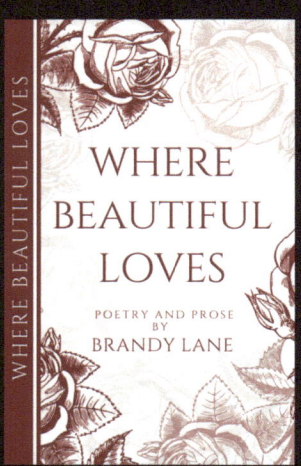
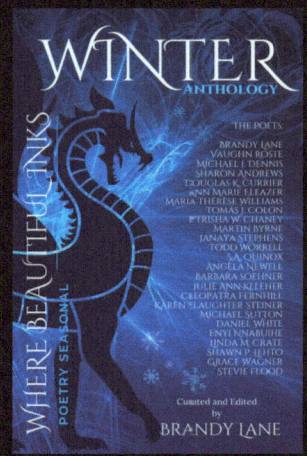
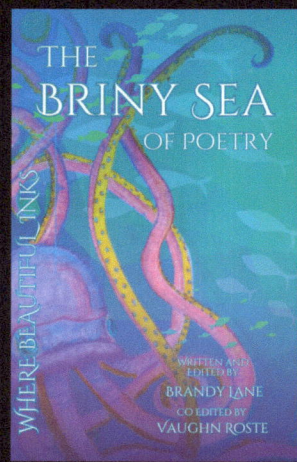

In the Works

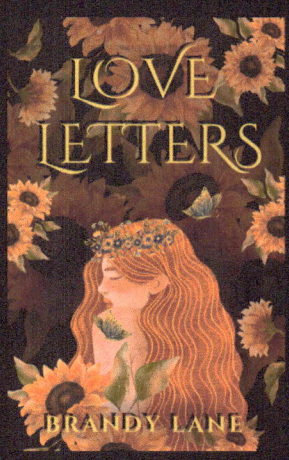